Our Prayers and Praise

The Order for Daily Morning Prayer and

The Order for the Administration

of the Lord's Supper

OR

Holy Communion

WITH SIMPLIFIED RUBRICS AND EXPLANATORY NOTES

Together with Notes on the Church Year

AND

The Collects to Be Used Throughout the Year

THE SEABURY PRESS · NEW YORK

THIS BOOK BELONGS TO

Thomas Alexander Lynch Pennington

I was baptized on... *10 November 1968*

in... *St. Paul's Episcopal Church*
Flint Michigan

TO THE OWNER OF THIS BOOK

This is a prayer book. It was made for you. You can use
it when you go to church. You can use it in your church
school class and at home. This book has parts of the Book
of Common Prayer in it. It also has parts written just for
you. These parts explain about Morning Prayer and Holy
Communion. They also tell you about the Church Year.
The page numbers of this book look like this: [13]. The
numbers without brackets [ ], which look like this: 7, are
the same as the page numbers in the Prayer Book.

LIBRARY OF CONGRESS CATALOGUE CARD NUMBER: 57–8341
SPECIAL CONTENTS © 1957 BY THE SEABURY PRESS, INCORPORATED
PRINTED IN THE UNITED STATES OF AMERICA

Fifth Printing, 1967

Morning Prayer

Morning Prayer

Many people thank God every morning when they get up. They thank Him for giving them another day of work and play. They ask God to watch over them in all they say and do. So, too, whenever a group of Church people are together in the morning, they say prayers and thanksgivings and read the Bible. We call this service "Morning Prayer."

The Order for
Daily Morning Prayer

¶ *The Minister shall begin the Morning Prayer by reading one or more of the following Sentences of Scripture.*

THE LORD is in his holy temple: let all the earth keep silence before him. *Habakkuk 2: 20.*

I was glad when they said unto me, We will go into the house of the LORD. *Psalm 122: 1.*

Let the words of my mouth, and the meditation of my heart, be alway acceptable in thy sight, O LORD, my strength and my redeemer. *Psalm 19: 14.*

O send out thy light and thy truth, that they may lead me, and bring me unto thy holy hill, and to thy dwelling. *Psalm 43: 3.*

Thus saith the high and lofty One that inhabiteth eternity, whose name is Holy; I dwell in the high and holy place, with him also that is of a contrite and humble spirit, to revive the spirit of the humble, and to revive the heart of the contrite ones. *Isaiah 57: 15.*

The hour cometh, and now is, when the true worshippers shall worship the Father in spirit and in truth: for the Father seeketh such to worship him. *St. John 4: 23.*

Morning Prayer

Grace be unto you, and peace, from God our Father, and from the Lord Jesus Christ. *Philippians 1: 2.*

Advent. Repent ye; for the Kingdom of heaven is at hand. *St. Matthew 3: 2.*

Prepare ye the way of the LORD, make straight in the desert a highway for our God. *Isaiah 40: 3.*

Christmas. Behold, I bring you good tidings of great joy, which shall be to all people. For unto you is born this day in the city of David a Saviour, which is Christ the Lord. *St. Luke 2: 10, 11.*

Epiphany. From the rising of the sun even unto the going down of the same my Name shall be great among the Gentiles; and in every place incense shall be offered unto my Name, and a pure offering: for my Name shall be great among the heathen, saith the LORD of hosts. *Malachi 1: 11.*

Awake, awake; put on thy strength, O Zion; put on thy beautiful garments, O Jerusalem. *Isaiah 52: 1.*

Lent. Rend your heart, and not your garments, and turn unto the LORD your God: for he is gracious and merciful, slow to anger, and of great kindness, and repenteth him of the evil. *Joel 2: 13.*

The sacrifices of God are a broken spirit: a broken and a contrite heart, O God, thou wilt not despise. *Psalm 51: 17.*

I will arise and go to my father, and will say unto him, Father, I have sinned against heaven, and before thee, and am no more worthy to be called thy son. *St. Luke 15: 18, 19.*

Good Friday. Is it nothing to you, all ye that pass by? behold, and see if there be any sorrow like unto my sorrow which is done unto me, wherewith the LORD hath afflicted me. *Lamentations 1: 12.*

In whom we have redemption through his blood, the forgiveness of sins, according to the riches of his grace. *Ephesians 1: 7.*

Morning Prayer

Easter. He is risen. The Lord is risen indeed. *St. Mark 16: 6; St. Luke 24: 34.*

This is the day which the LORD hath made; we will rejoice and be glad in it. *Psalm 118: 24.*

Ascension. Seeing that we have a great High Priest, that is passed into the heavens, Jesus the Son of God, let us come boldly unto the throne of grace, that we may obtain mercy, and find grace to help in time of need. *Hebrews 4: 14, 16.*

Whitsunday. Ye shall receive power, after that the Holy Ghost is come upon you: and ye shall be witnesses unto me both in Jerusalem, and in all Judæa, and in Samaria, and unto the uttermost part of the earth. *Acts 1: 8.*

Because ye are sons, God hath sent forth the Spirit of his Son into your hearts, crying, Abba, Father. *Galatians 4: 6.*

Trinity Sunday. Holy, holy, holy, Lord God Almighty, which was, and is, and is to come. *Revelation 4: 8.*

Thanksgiving Day. Honour the LORD with thy substance, and with the first-fruits of all thine increase: so shall thy barns be filled with plenty, and thy presses shall burst out with new wine. *Proverbs 3: 9, 10.*

The LORD by wisdom hath founded the earth; by understanding hath he established the heavens. By his knowledge the depths are broken up, and the clouds drop down the dew. *Proverbs 3: 19, 20.*

Morning Prayer

℣ *Then the Minister shall say,*

LET us humbly confess our sins unto Almighty God.

A General Confession.

℣ *To be said by everyone together, kneeling.*

ALMIGHTY and most merciful Father; We have erred, and strayed from thy ways like lost sheep. We have followed too much the devices and desires of our own hearts. We have offended against thy holy laws. We have left undone those things which we ought to have done; And we have done those things which we ought not to have done; And there is no health in us. But thou, O Lord, have mercy upon us, miserable offenders. Spare thou those, O God, who confess their faults. Restore thou those who are penitent; According to thy promises declared unto mankind In Christ Jesus our Lord. And grant, O most merciful Father, for his sake; That we may hereafter live a godly, righteous, and sober life, To the glory of thy holy Name. Amen.

6

A General Confession

When we love someone, we are happy in the person's company. This is true whether we are grownups or children. But we often make each other unhappy by being selfish, or mean and rude. For example, sometimes we say "No" when we are asked to help. When something like this happens, the only way we can be happy with one another again is to admit that we were wrong, hope to be forgiven, and plan to do better.

God loves us, too. He wants us to be happy in His company. But when we are selfish, do mean things or say ugly words, we displease Him. Our selfishness is what we call sin. We cannot be happy in God's company again until we tell Him we are truly sorry for our sin. When we tell Him this, we are making a confession to Him.

Everyone acts badly from time to time, and everyone is in need of confessing this to God. We call the Confession "general" because we say it together, with the Minister.

The Absolution

When we do something we are sorry for, and show that we are sorry, we hope that those who love us will forgive us. If they did not love us, they would not forgive us. But even when we are forgiven, those who love us want us to try our best not to be so mean and selfish again.

God forgives us our sins, too, because He loves us. If we are truly sorry, and promise to try our best to be kind and loving and helpful, God will also help us keep that promise. This is what the Priest tells us while we are still kneeling after our confession. We call the Priest's words the Absolution.

Morning Prayer

The Declaration of Absolution, or Remission of Sins.

ALMIGHTY God, the Father of our Lord Jesus Christ, who desireth not the death of a sinner, but rather that he may turn from his wickedness and live, hath given power, and commandment, to his Ministers, to declare and pronounce to his people, being penitent, the Absolution and Remission of their sins. He pardoneth and absolveth all those who truly repent, and unfeignedly believe his holy Gospel.

Wherefore let us beseech him to grant us true repentance, and his Holy Spirit, that those things may please him which we do at this present; and that the rest of our life hereafter may be pure and holy; so that at the last we may come to his eternal joy; through Jesus Christ our Lord. *Amen.*

❡ *To be said by everyone together, kneeling.*

OUR Father, who art in heaven, Hallowed be thy Name. Thy kingdom come. Thy will be done, On earth as it is in heaven. Give us this day our daily bread. And forgive us our trespasses, As we forgive those who trespass against us. And lead us not into temptation, But deliver us from evil. For thine is the kingdom, and the power, and the glory, for ever and ever. Amen.

❡ *Then he shall say,*

O Lord, open thou our lips.

Answer. And our mouth shall show forth thy praise.

Morning Prayer

Glory be to the Father, and to the Son, and to the Holy Ghost;

Answer. As it was in the beginning, is now, and ever shall be, world without end. Amen.

Minister. Praise ye the Lord.

Answer. The Lord's Name be praised.

❡ *Then shall be said or sung the Venite.*

The Venite

The Absolution tells us that God loves us, and this makes us so happy we want to sing. That is why we sing the Venite. The word "venite" is Latin for "O come," the first two words of this song.

In the Venite we thank God for making us His children. We thank Him for placing us in the wonderful world He has made. We thank Him for His constant care of us. He feeds us and helps us. He protects us from harm. We also remember that He expects us to obey Him.

8

Morning Prayer

Venite, exultemus Domino.

O COME, let us sing unto the LORD; * let us heartily rejoice in the strength of our salvation.

Let us come before his presence with thanksgiving; * and show ourselves glad in him with psalms.

For the LORD is a great God; * and a great King above all gods.

In his hand are all the corners of the earth; * and the strength of the hills is his also.

The sea is his, and he made it; * and his hands prepared the dry land.

O come, let us worship and fall down, * and kneel before the LORD our Maker.

For he is the Lord our God; * and we are the people of his pasture, and the sheep of his hand.

O worship the LORD in the beauty of holiness; * let the whole earth stand in awe of him.

For he cometh, for he cometh to judge the earth; * and with righteousness to judge the world, and the peoples with his truth.

¶ *Then shall follow one or more of the Psalms from the Prayer Book. At the end of the reading of each Psalm, the Gloria Patri shall be said or sung. The Gloria Patri may also be said or sung at the end of the Venite, Benedictus es, Benedictus, and the Jubilate.*

G LORY be to the Father, and to the Son, * and to the Holy Ghost;

As it was in the beginning, is now, and ever shall be, * world without end. Amen.

¶ *Then shall be read the First Lesson.*

Morning Prayer

❡ *Here shall be said or sung the following Hymn.*

Te Deum laudamus.

WE praise thee, O God; we acknowledge thee to be the Lord.

All the earth doth worship thee, the Father everlasting.

To thee all Angels cry aloud; the Heavens, and all the Powers therein;

To thee Cherubim and Seraphim continually do cry,

Holy, Holy, Holy, Lord God of Sabaoth;

Heaven and earth are full of the Majesty of thy glory.

The glorious company of the Apostles praise thee.

The goodly fellowship of the Prophets praise thee.

The noble army of Martyrs praise thee.

The holy Church throughout all the world doth acknowledge thee;

The Father, of an infinite Majesty;

Thine adorable, true, and only Son;

Also the Holy Ghost, the Comforter.

THOU art the King of Glory, O Christ.

Thou art the everlasting Son of the Father.

When thou tookest upon thee to deliver man, thou didst humble thyself to be born of a Virgin.

When thou hadst overcome the sharpness of death, thou didst open the Kingdom of Heaven to all believers.

Thou sittest at the right hand of God, in the glory of the Father.

We believe that thou shalt come to be our Judge.

We therefore pray thee, help thy servants, whom thou hast redeemed with thy precious blood.

The Lessons

After we have finished the Venite and a Psalm or Psalms, we sit down while the Minister reads to us from the Bible. He reads two Lessons. The First Lesson is from the Old Testament. The Second Lesson is from the New Testament.

When we listen to the Lessons, we learn about God. How He made the world and everything in it. How He constantly loves and cares for all people. How He promises happiness to all who obey Him. How He sent His Son, Jesus Christ, to be our Saviour. How He sent forth Christ's companions into all the world to tell the people about God's love for them.

The Canticles

After each of the Lessons has been read to us, we stand up and sing another song called a canticle. The word "canticle" means "song." In Morning Prayer there are several of these songs. We choose one to sing after each Lesson.

The canticles help us to thank God for making us and all the world, and for sending Jesus to us to be our Saviour. Like the Venite, the canticles remind us of how much God cares for us, and how He watches over us day by day.

Make them to be numbered with thy Saints, in glory everlasting.

O LORD, save thy people, and bless thine heritage. Govern them, and lift them up for ever.

Day by day we magnify thee;

And we worship thy Name ever, world without end.

Vouchsafe, O Lord, to keep us this day without sin.

O Lord, have mercy upon us, have mercy upon us.

O Lord, let thy mercy be upon us, as our trust is in thee.

O Lord, in thee have I trusted; let me never be confounded.

¶ *Or this Canticle.*

Benedictus es, Domine.

B LESSED art thou, O Lord God of our fathers: * praised and exalted above all for ever.

Blessed art thou for the Name of thy Majesty: * praised and exalted above all for ever.

Blessed art thou in the temple of thy holiness: * praised and exalted above all for ever.

Blessed art thou that beholdest the depths, and dwellest between the Cherubim: * praised and exalted above all for ever.

Blessed art thou on the glorious throne of thy kingdom: * praised and exalted above all for ever.

Blessed art thou in the firmament of heaven: * praised and exalted above all for ever.

¶ *Or this Canticle.*

Benedicite, omnia opera Domini.

O ALL ye Works of the Lord, bless ye the Lord: * praise him, and magnify him for ever.

Morning Prayer

O ye Angels of the Lord, bless ye the Lord: * praise him, and magnify him for ever.

O YE Heavens, bless ye the Lord: * praise him, and magnify him for ever.

O ye Waters that be above the firmament, bless ye the Lord: * praise him, and magnify him for ever.

O all ye Powers of the Lord, bless ye the Lord: * praise him, and magnify him for ever.

O ye Sun and Moon, bless ye the Lord: * praise him, and magnify him for ever.

O ye Stars of heaven, bless ye the Lord: * praise him, and magnify him for ever.

O ye Showers and Dew, bless ye the Lord: * praise him, and magnify him for ever.

O ye Winds of God, bless ye the Lord: * praise him, and magnify him for ever.

O ye Fire and Heat, bless ye the Lord: * praise him, and magnify him for ever.

O ye Winter and Summer, bless ye the Lord: * praise him, and magnify him for ever.

O ye Dews and Frosts, bless ye the Lord: * praise him, and magnify him for ever.

O ye Frost and Cold, bless ye the Lord: * praise him, and magnify him for ever.

O ye Ice and Snow, bless ye the Lord: * praise him, and magnify him for ever.

O ye Nights and Days, bless ye the Lord: * praise him, and magnify him for ever.

O ye Light and Darkness, bless ye the Lord: * praise him, and magnify him for ever.

O ye Lightnings and Clouds, bless ye the Lord: * praise him, and magnify him for ever.

Morning Prayer

O LET the Earth bless the Lord: * yea, let it praise him and magnify him for ever.

O ye Mountains and Hills, bless ye the Lord: * praise him, and magnify him for ever.

O all ye Green Things upon the earth, bless ye the Lord: * praise him, and magnify him for ever.

O ye Wells, bless ye the Lord: * praise him, and magnify him for ever.

O ye Seas and Floods, bless ye the Lord: * praise him, and magnify him for ever.

O ye Whales, and all that move in the waters, bless ye the Lord: * praise him, and magnify him for ever.

O all ye Fowls of the air, bless ye the Lord: * praise him, and magnify him for ever.

O all ye Beasts and Cattle, bless ye the Lord: * praise him, and magnify him for ever.

O ye Children of Men, bless ye the Lord: * praise him, and magnify him for ever.

O LET Israel bless the Lord: * praise him, and magnify him for ever.

O ye Priests of the Lord, bless ye the Lord: * praise him, and magnify him for ever.

O ye Servants of the Lord, bless ye the Lord: * praise him, and magnify him for ever.

O ye Spirits and Souls of the Righteous, bless ye the Lord: * praise him, and magnify him for ever.

O ye holy and humble Men of heart, bless ye the Lord: * praise him, and magnify him for ever.

LET us bless the Father, and the Son, and the Holy Ghost: * praise him, and magnify him for ever.

Morning Prayer

❡ Then shall be read the Second Lesson.
❡ And after that shall be sung or said the Hymn following.

Benedictus. St. Luke 1: 68.

BLESSED be the Lord God of Israel; * for he hath visited and redeemed his people;

And hath raised up a mighty salvation for us, * in the house of his servant David;

As he spake by the mouth of his holy Prophets, * which have been since the world began;

That we should be saved from our enemies, * and from the hand of all that hate us.

To perform the mercy promised to our forefathers, * and to remember his holy covenant;

To perform the oath which he sware to our forefather Abraham, * that he would give us;

That we being delivered out of the hand of our enemies * might serve him without fear;

In holiness and righteousness before him, * all the days of our life.

And thou, child, shalt be called the prophet of the Highest: * for thou shalt go before the face of the Lord to prepare his ways;

To give knowledge of salvation unto his people * for the remission of their sins,

Through the tender mercy of our God; * whereby the day-spring from on high hath visited us;

To give light to them that sit in darkness, and in the shadow of death, * and to guide our feet into the way of peace.

Morning Prayer

¶ *Or this Psalm.*

Jubilate Deo. Psalm 100.

O BE joyful in the LORD, all ye lands: * serve the LORD with gladness, and come before his presence with a song.

Be ye sure that the LORD he is God; it is he that hath made us, and not we ourselves; * we are his people, and the sheep of his pasture.

O go your way into his gates with thanksgiving, and into his courts with praise; * be thankful unto him, and speak good of his Name.

For the LORD is gracious, his mercy is everlasting; * and his truth endureth from generation to generation.

¶ *Then shall be said the Apostles' Creed by the Minister and the People, standing.*

I BELIEVE in God the Father Almighty, Maker of heaven and earth:

And in Jesus Christ his only Son our Lord: Who was conceived by the Holy Ghost, Born of the Virgin Mary: Suffered under Pontius Pilate, Was crucified, dead, and buried: He descended into hell; The third day he rose again from the dead: He ascended into heaven, And sitteth on the right hand of God the Father Almighty: From thence he shall come to judge the quick and the dead.

I believe in the Holy Ghost: The holy Catholic Church; The Communion of Saints: The Forgiveness of sins: The Resurrection of the body: And the Life everlasting. Amen.

¶ *Or the Creed commonly called the Nicene.*

I BELIEVE in one God the Father Almighty, Maker of heaven and earth, And of all things visible and invisible:

Morning Prayer

And in one Lord Jesus Christ, the only-begotten Son of God; Begotten of his Father before all worlds, God of God, Light of Light, Very God of very God; Begotten, not made; Being of one substance with the Father; By whom all things were made: Who for us men and for our salvation came down from heaven, And was incarnate by the Holy Ghost of the Virgin Mary, And was made man: And was crucified also for us under Pontius Pilate; He suffered and was buried: And the third day he rose again according to the Scriptures: And ascended into heaven, And sitteth on the right hand of the Father: And he shall come again, with glory, to judge both the quick and the dead; Whose kingdom shall have no end.

And I believe in the Holy Ghost, The Lord, and Giver of Life, Who proceedeth from the Father and the Son; Who with the Father and the Son together is worshipped and glorified; Who spake by the Prophets: And I believe one Catholic and Apostolic Church: I acknowledge one Baptism for the remission of sins: And I look for the Resurrection of the dead: And the Life of the world to come. Amen.

¶ Then the Minister shall say,

The Lord be with you.
Answer. And with thy spirit.
Minister. Let us pray.

¶ Here, if it has not already been said, shall follow the Lord's Prayer.

Minister. O Lord, show thy mercy upon us.
Answer. And grant us thy salvation.
Minister. O God, make clean our hearts within us.
Answer. And take not thy Holy Spirit from us.

The Apostles' Creed

When we have finished our songs, we say the Apostles' Creed together. The word "creed" comes from the Latin word "credo," which is the first word of the Creed in Latin. It means "I believe." This Creed is called the Apostles' Creed because it contains what was taught us by Jesus' companions, the apostles.

The Creed is our promise of loyalty to God who is our Maker, our Saviour, and our Guide. When we were baptized, and made members of the Church, our parents and godparents made this promise of loyalty for us. They also promised to help us follow this pledge as members of the Church.

The Prayers

After the Creed, we all kneel once again, to say our prayers. The first prayer the Minister reads is the Collect (or prayer) for the Day. You will find the Collects for the Day in this book beginning on page 68. After the Minister reads the Collect for the Day, he sometimes reads other special Collects. Then he reads other prayers asking God to bless us and all people in the world.

Two prayers are always read: one for peace and one for grace. In these two prayers, we ask God to take care of us during the day. We ask Him to protect us from everything that hurts us. And we ask Him to help us to be good and strong against all the things that tempt us to be selfish and unloving.

Morning Prayer

❡ *Here shall be read the Collect for the Day, followed by a Collect for Peace and a Collect for Grace.*

A Collect for Peace.

O GOD, who art the author of peace and lover of concord, in knowledge of whom standeth our eternal life, whose service is perfect freedom; Defend us thy humble servants in all assaults of our enemies; that we, surely trusting in thy defence, may not fear the power of any adversaries, through the might of Jesus Christ our Lord. *Amen.*

A Collect for Grace.

O LORD, our heavenly Father, Almighty and everlasting God, who hast safely brought us to the beginning of this day; Defend us in the same with thy mighty power; and grant that this day we fall into no sin, neither run into any kind of danger; but that all our doings, being ordered by thy governance, may be righteous in thy sight; through Jesus Christ our Lord. *Amen.*

❡ *Then the following Prayers, or others from the Prayer Book, may be said.*

A Prayer for The President of the United States, and all in Civil Authority.

O LORD, our heavenly Father, the high and mighty Ruler of the universe, who dost from thy throne behold all the dwellers upon earth; Most heartily we beseech thee, with thy favour to behold and bless thy servant THE PRESIDENT OF THE UNITED STATES, and all others in authority; and so replenish them with the grace of thy Holy Spirit, that they may always incline to thy will, and walk in thy way.

Endue them plenteously with heavenly gifts; grant them in health and prosperity long to live; and finally, after this life, to attain everlasting joy and felicity; through Jesus Christ our Lord. *Amen.*

¶ *Or this.*

O LORD our Governor, whose glory is in all the world; We commend this nation to thy merciful care, that being guided by thy Providence, we may dwell secure in thy peace. Grant to THE PRESIDENT OF THE UNITED STATES, and to all in authority, wisdom and strength to know and to do thy will. Fill them with the love of truth and righteousness; and make them ever mindful of their calling to serve this people in thy fear; through Jesus Christ our Lord, who liveth and reigneth with thee and the Holy Ghost, one God, world without end. *Amen.*

A Prayer for the Clergy and People.

A LMIGHTY and everlasting God, from whom cometh every good and perfect gift; Send down upon our Bishops, and other Clergy, and upon the Congregations committed to their charge, the healthful Spirit of thy grace; and, that they may truly please thee, pour upon them the continual dew of thy blessing. Grant this, O Lord, for the honour of our Advocate and Mediator, Jesus Christ. *Amen.*

A Prayer for all Conditions of Men.

O GOD, the Creator and Preserver of all mankind, we humbly beseech thee for all sorts and conditions of men; that thou wouldest be pleased to make thy ways known unto them, thy saving health unto all nations. More especially we pray for thy holy Church universal; that it may be so guided and governed by thy good Spirit, that all who profess and call themselves Christians may be led into the way of truth, and hold the faith in unity of spirit, in the bond of peace, and in righteousness of life. Finally, we commend to thy fatherly goodness all those who are any ways afflicted, or distressed, in mind, body, or estate; that it may please thee to comfort and relieve them, according to their several necessities; giving them patience under their sufferings, and a happy issue out of all their afflictions. And this we beg for Jesus Christ's sake. *Amen.*

A General Thanksgiving.

ALMIGHTY God, Father of all mercies, we, thine unworthy servants, do give thee most humble and hearty thanks for all thy goodness and loving-kindness to us, and to all men. We bless thee for our creation, preservation, and all the blessings of this life; but above all, for thine inestimable love in the redemption of the world by our Lord Jesus Christ; for the means of grace, and for the hope of glory. And, we beseech thee, give us that due sense of all thy mercies, that our hearts may be unfeignedly thankful; and that we show forth thy praise, not only with our lips, but in our lives, by giving up our selves to thy service, and by walking before thee in holiness and righteousness all our days; through Jesus Christ our Lord, to whom, with thee and the Holy Ghost, be all honour and glory, world without end. *Amen.*

❡ NOTE, *That the General Thanksgiving may be said by the Congregation with the Minister.*

Morning Prayer

A Prayer of St. Chrysostom.

ALMIGHTY God, who hast given us grace at this time with one accord to make our common supplications unto thee; and dost promise that when two or three are gathered together in thy Name thou wilt grant their requests; Fulfil now, O Lord, the desires and petitions of thy servants, as may be most expedient for them; granting us in this world knowledge of thy truth, and in the world to come life everlasting. *Amen.*

The Grace. 2 Corinthians 13 : 14.

THE grace of our Lord Jesus Christ, and the love of God, and the fellowship of the Holy Ghost, be with us all evermore. *Amen.*

Here ends the Order of Morning Prayer.

The Holy Communion

The Holy Communion

The earliest name for the Holy Communion is Eucharist. The word "eucharist" means "thanksgiving." In this service we give thanks to God for sending His Son Jesus Christ. We do this by acting out His coming to us as Saviour. We know that He is present with us at the family table in His Church, as He is in all parts of our lives. Yet in this service He is present with us in a very special way, for in it we do what Jesus asked His disciples to do in memory of Him.

The Order for

The Administration of the Lord's Supper

or

Holy Communion

❡ *At the Communion-time the Holy Table shall have upon it a fair white linen cloth. The Priest shall stand before the Holy Table. The People shall kneel.*

The Collect.

ALMIGHTY God, unto whom all hearts are open, all desires known, and from whom no secrets are hid; Cleanse the thoughts of our hearts by the inspiration of thy Holy Spirit, that we may perfectly love thee, and worthily magnify thy holy Name; through Christ our Lord. *Amen.*

❡ *Then shall the Priest read the Ten Commandments or the Summary of the Law, or both.*

Holy Communion

The Decalogue.

GOD spake these words, and said:
I am the LORD thy God; Thou shalt have none other gods but me.

Lord, have mercy upon us, and incline our hearts to keep this law.

Thou shalt not make to thyself any graven image, nor the likeness of any thing that is in heaven above, or in the earth beneath, or in the water under the earth; thou shalt not bow down to them, nor worship them;

Lord, have mercy upon us, and incline our hearts to keep this law.

Thou shalt not take the Name of the LORD thy God in vain;

Lord, have mercy upon us, and incline our hearts to keep this law.

Remember that thou keep holy the Sabbath-day.

Lord, have mercy upon us, and incline our hearts to keep this law.

The Commandments

In our family we follow certain rules of behaviour. If we did not do so, we would be uncomfortable because we would not know what was expected of us. So it is in God's world. God is our Father, and by His commandments we know what he expects of us as His children.

The first four of the Ten Commandments tell us our duty towards God. The last six tell us our duty towards others. The Ten Commandments are sometimes called the Decalogue.

The Summary of the Law

When the Lord Jesus was asked which of God's commandments was the greatest, He replied that all of God's commandments for His children could be summed up in a few words: To love God with all your heart and soul and mind, and to love your neighbour as yourself. This is called the Summary of the Law.

Holy Communion

Honour thy father and thy mother;
Lord, have mercy upon us, and incline our hearts to keep this law.
Thou shalt do no murder.
Lord, have mercy upon us, and incline our hearts to keep this law.
Thou shalt not commit adultery.
Lord, have mercy upon us, and incline our hearts to keep this law.
Thou shalt not steal.
Lord, have mercy upon us, and incline our hearts to keep this law.
Thou shalt not bear false witness against thy neighbour.
Lord, have mercy upon us, and incline our hearts to keep this law.
Thou shalt not covet.
Lord, have mercy upon us, and write all these thy laws in our hearts, we beseech thee.

¶ Then may the Priest say,

Hear what our Lord Jesus Christ saith.

THOU shalt love the Lord thy God with all thy heart, and with all thy soul, and with all thy mind. This is the first and great commandment. And the second is like unto it; Thou shalt love thy neighbour as thyself. On these two commandments hang all the Law and the Prophets.

¶ Here, if the Decalogue has been omitted, shall be said,

Holy Communion

Lord, have mercy upon us.
Christ, have mercy upon us.
Lord, have mercy upon us.

℣ *Then the Priest may say,*

O ALMIGHTY Lord, and everlasting God, vouchsafe, we beseech thee, to direct, sanctify, and govern, both our hearts and bodies, in the ways of thy laws, and in the works of thy commandments; that, through thy most mighty protection, both here and ever, we may be preserved in body and soul; through our Lord and Saviour Jesus Christ. *Amen.*

℣ *Here shall be said,*

The Lord be with you.
Answer. And with thy spirit.
Minister. Let us pray.

℣ *Then shall the Priest say the Collect of the Day. After the Collect shall be read the Epistle.*
℣ *Here may be sung a Hymn or an Anthem.*
℣ *Then, all the People standing, the Minister shall read the Gospel. After the Gospel is announced and before it is read all shall say,*

Glory be to thee, O Lord.

℣ *And after the Gospel may be said,*

Praise be to thee, O Christ.

℣ *Then shall be said the Nicene Creed, or the Apostles' Creed, except on certain occasions.*

The Epistle and Gospel

Each Sunday and Holy Day in the Church Year has two special readings from the Bible. These readings are called the Epistle and the Gospel.

An epistle is a letter. The Epistle is usually taken from one of the New Testament Epistles. Saint Paul wrote many of these. They were sent to churches in cities around the Mediterranean Sea. The letters were saved so that they could be read over and over again.

The word "gospel" means "good news." In the New Testament there are four books called Gospels that tell us what Jesus did and said. They are the most important books in the world. The Gospel for the day is a lesson read from one of these four Gospels.

The Nicene Creed

The Nicene Creed is a statement of what we believe about God and the things He has done for us. It was written down by the bishops of the early Church so that all the world might know what Christians believe. We stand and say it together as a promise of loyalty to God who is our Maker, our Saviour, and our Guide.

The Nicene Creed is longer than the Apostles' Creed, but both Creeds talk about the same things. The name "Nicene" comes from the city of Nicaea, in Asia Minor, where the first effort was made to write down this Creed.

Holy Communion

I BELIEVE in one God the Father Almighty, Maker of heaven and earth, And of all things visible and invisible:

And in one Lord Jesus Christ, the only-begotten Son of God; Begotten of his Father before all worlds, God of God, Light of Light, Very God of very God; Begotten, not made; Being of one substance with the Father; By whom all things were made: Who for us men and for our salvation came down from heaven, And was incarnate by the Holy Ghost of the Virgin Mary, And was made man: And was crucified also for us under Pontius Pilate; He suffered and was buried: And the third day he rose again according to the Scriptures: And ascended into heaven, And sitteth on the right hand of the Father: And he shall come again, with glory, to judge both the quick and the dead; Whose kingdom shall have no end.

And I believe in the Holy Ghost, The Lord, and Giver of Life, Who proceedeth from the Father and the Son; Who with the Father and the Son together is worshipped and glorified; Who spake by the Prophets: And I believe one Catholic and Apostolic Church: I acknowledge one Baptism for the remission of sins: And I look for the Resurrection of the dead: And the Life of the world to come. Amen.

℣ *Then follows the Sermon. After the Sermon the Priest shall begin the Offertory, saying one or more of the following Sentences.*

Holy Communion

REMEMBER the words of the Lord Jesus, how he said, It is more blessed to give than to receive. *Acts 20: 35.*

Let your light so shine before men, that they may see your good works, and glorify your Father which is in heaven. *St. Matthew 5: 16.*

Lay not up for yourselves treasures upon earth, where moth and rust doth corrupt, and where thieves break through and steal: but lay up for yourselves treasures in heaven, where neither moth nor rust doth corrupt, and where thieves do not break through nor steal. *St. Matthew 6: 19, 20.*

Not every one that saith unto me, Lord, Lord, shall enter into the kingdom of heaven; but he that doeth the will of my Father which is in heaven. *St. Matthew 7: 21.*

He that soweth little shall reap little; and he that soweth plenteously shall reap plenteously. Let every man do according as he is disposed in his heart, not grudgingly, or of necessity; for God loveth a cheerful giver. *2 Corinthians 9: 6, 7.*

While we have time, let us do good unto all men; and especially unto them that are of the household of faith. *Galatians 6: 10.*

God is not unrighteous, that he will forget your works, and labour that proceedeth of love; which love ye have showed for his Name's sake, who have ministered unto the saints, and yet do minister. *Hebrews 6: 10.*

To do good, and to distribute, forget not; for with such sacrifices God is well pleased. *Hebrews 13: 16.*

Whoso hath this world's good, and seeth his brother have need, and shutteth up his compassion from him, how dwelleth the love of God in him? *1 St. John 3: 17.*

Be merciful after thy power. If thou hast much, give plenteously; if thou hast little, do thy diligence gladly to give of that little: for so gatherest thou thyself a good reward in the day of necessity. *Tobit 4: 8, 9.*

The Offertory

We all enjoy giving things to people we love. In the part of the Holy Communion called the Offertory, we offer to God two kinds of presents from all the things that He has given us. One of these offerings is a gift of our money. This money will be used to spread the Good News about God, who loves us and all people.

The other offering in the Holy Communion is the bread and the wine. We make the bread and the wine from the good things God has given us in His creation. So we offer these gifts to Him that He may bless them and us and all our life.

Holy Communion

And the King shall answer and say unto them, Verily I say unto you, Inasmuch as ye have done it unto one of the least of these my brethren, ye have done it unto me. *St. Matthew 25: 40.*

How then shall they call on him in whom they have not believed? and how shall they believe in him of whom they have not heard? and how shall they hear without a preacher? and how shall they preach, except they be sent? *Romans 10: 14, 15.*

Jesus said unto them, The harvest truly is plenteous, but the labourers are few: pray ye therefore the Lord of the harvest, that he send forth labourers into his harvest. *St. Luke 10: 2.*

Ye shall not appear before the LORD empty; every man shall give as he is able, according to the blessing of the LORD thy God which he hath given thee. *Deuteronomy 16: 16, 17.*

Thine, O LORD, is the greatness, and the power, and the glory, and the victory, and the majesty: for all that is in the heaven and in the earth is thine; thine is the kingdom, O LORD, and thou art exalted as head above all. *1 Chronicles 29: 11.*

All things come of thee, O LORD, and of thine own have we given thee. *1 Chronicles 29: 14.*

¶ *The Offerings of the People shall be received and shall be brought to the Priest who shall humbly present and place them upon the Holy Table.*

¶ *And the Priest shall then offer, and shall place upon the Holy Table, the Bread and the Wine.*

¶ *When the Offering of money and of the Bread and Wine are being received and presented, there may be sung a Hymn or an Anthem.*

Holy Communion

❡ *Here the Priest may ask the intercessions of the Congregation for any who have desired the prayers of the Church.*

❡ *Then shall the Priest say,*

Let us pray for the whole state of Christ's Church.

ALMIGHTY and everliving God, who by thy holy Apostle hast taught us to make prayers, and supplications, and to give thanks for all men; We humbly beseech thee most mercifully to accept our [*alms and*] oblations, and to receive these our prayers, which we offer unto thy Divine Majesty; beseeching thee to inspire continually the Universal Church with the spirit of truth, unity, and concord: And grant that all those who do confess thy holy Name may agree in the truth of thy holy Word, and live in unity and godly love.

We beseech thee also, so to direct and dispose the hearts of all Christian Rulers, that they may truly and impartially administer justice, to the punishment of wickedness and vice, and to the maintenance of thy true religion, and virtue.

Give grace, O heavenly Father, to all Bishops and other Ministers, that they may, both by their life and doctrine, set forth thy true and lively Word, and rightly and duly administer thy holy Sacraments.

And to all thy People give thy heavenly grace; and especially to this congregation here present; that, with meek heart and due reverence, they may hear, and receive thy holy Word; truly serving thee in holiness and righteousness all the days of their life.

And we most humbly beseech thee, of thy goodness, O Lord, to comfort and succour all those who, in this transitory life, are in trouble, sorrow, need, sickness, or any other adversity.

And we also bless thy holy Name for all thy servants departed this life in thy faith and fear; beseeching thee to

The Prayer for the Church

In our prayers at bedtime we remember our family and our friends, both those who are near us and those who are far away. This prayer is like that. It is a prayer for the whole Christian family. In it we ask God to accept our offerings to Him and our prayers for all people. We pray especially for those who are sick and in need. And we do not forget to pray for those we love who have died and who are still members of God's family, the Church.

The Invitation and Confession

When we have been mean and selfish, or have done some other wrong to a person, we need to do three things to make everything right again. One is to admit that we have been wrong and to be sorry. Another is to feel kindly towards the person we have hurt. The third is to plan to do better with God's help.

The General Confession is the prayer we say aloud together when we are telling God we have done wrong and need His forgiveness. This confession is like the one we say together in Morning Prayer.

grant them continual growth in thy love and service, and to give us grace so to follow their good examples, that with them we may be partakers of thy heavenly kingdom. Grant this, O Father, for Jesus Christ's sake, our only Mediator and Advocate. *Amen.*

¶ *Then shall the Priest say,*

YE who do truly and earnestly repent you of your sins, and are in love and charity with your neighbours, and intend to lead a new life, following the commandments of God, and walking from henceforth in his holy ways; Draw near with faith, and take this holy Sacrament to your comfort; and make your humble confession to Almighty God, devoutly kneeling.

¶ *Then shall this General Confession be made, everyone humbly kneeling.*

ALMIGHTY God, Father of our Lord Jesus Christ, Maker of all things, Judge of all men; We acknowledge and bewail our manifold sins and wickedness, Which we, from time to time, most grievously have committed, By thought, word, and deed, Against thy Divine Majesty, Provoking most justly thy wrath and indignation against us. We do earnestly repent, And are heartily sorry for these our misdoings; The remembrance of them is grievous unto us; The burden of them is intolerable. Have mercy upon us, Have mercy upon us, most merciful Father; For thy Son our Lord Jesus Christ's sake, Forgive us all that is past; And grant that we may ever hereafter Serve and please thee In newness of life, To the honour and glory of thy Name; Through Jesus Christ our Lord. Amen.

¶ *Then shall the Priest (the Bishop if he be present) stand up, and turning to the People, say,*

Holy Communion

ALMIGHTY God, our heavenly Father, who of his great mercy hath promised forgiveness of sins to all those who with hearty repentance and true faith turn unto him; Have mercy upon you; pardon and deliver you from all your sins; confirm and strengthen you in all goodness; and bring you to everlasting life; through Jesus Christ our Lord. *Amen.*

¶ *Then shall the Priest say,*

Hear what comfortable words our Saviour Christ saith unto all who truly turn to him.

COME unto me, all ye that travail and are heavy laden, and I will refresh you. *St. Matthew 11: 28.*

So God loved the world, that he gave his only-begotten Son, to the end that all that believe in him should not perish, but have everlasting life. *St. John 3: 16.*

Hear also what Saint Paul saith.

This is a true saying, and worthy of all men to be received, That Christ Jesus came into the world to save sinners. *1 Timothy 1: 15.*

Hear also what Saint John saith.

If any man sin, we have an Advocate with the Father, Jesus Christ the righteous; and he is the Propitiation for our sins. *1 St. John 2: 1, 2.*

¶ *After which the Priest shall proceed, saying,*

Lift up your hearts.
Answer. We lift them up unto the Lord.
Priest. Let us give thanks unto our Lord God.
Answer. It is meet and right so to do.

¶ *Then shall the Priest turn to the Holy Table, and say,*

IT is very meet, right, and our bounden duty, that we should at all times, and in all places, give thanks unto thee, O Lord, Holy Father, Almighty, Everlasting God.

The Absolution and Comfortable Words

God is always ready to forgive us and to give us His strength. The Priest tells us this when he says the Absolution.

"Comfortable" here does not mean "cozy." It means "strengthening," "giving strength." If you were climbing up a steep hill and could not quite make the top, you would welcome, more than anything, someone with a strong arm to help you. This is what our Saviour Jesus Christ does. He comes to us in God's Name, wherever we are, and helps us.

The Sursum Corda

The central part of the service begins as the Priest calls us to lift up our hearts to God and give Him praise and thanks. (The Latin words "sursum corda" mean "lift up your hearts.") We reply, gladly, that we are indeed ready to do so. If we were asked to say in one word what our religion means, that word would be "thankfulness."

The Sanctus

Sometimes on a beautiful day we are so full of the joy of
being alive that we want to shout! The Sanctus is like that.
It does not ask for anything. It simply says thank you to
God for making such a wonderful world and for living in it
with us. (The word "sanctus" means "holy.")

Holy Communion

❡ *Here shall follow the Proper Preface, according to the Season, if one is specially appointed. If there is no Proper Preface, the Priest shall say or sing,*

THEREFORE with Angels and Archangels, and with all the company of heaven, we laud and magnify thy glorious Name; evermore praising thee, and saying,
HOLY, HOLY, HOLY, Lord God of *❡ Priest and People.* hosts, Heaven and earth are full of thy Glory: Glory be to thee, O Lord Most High. Amen.

PROPER PREFACES.

CHRISTMAS.

❡ *Upon Christmas Day, and seven days after.*

BECAUSE thou didst give Jesus Christ, thine only Son, to be born as at this time for us; who, by the operation of the Holy Ghost, was made very man, of the substance of the Virgin Mary his mother; and that without spot of sin, to make us clean from all sin.
Therefore with Angels, etc.

EPIPHANY.

❡ *Upon the Epiphany, and seven days after.*

THROUGH Jesus Christ our Lord; who, in substance of our mortal flesh, manifested forth his glory; that he might bring us out of darkness into his own glorious light.
Therefore with Angels, etc.

PURIFICATION, ANNUNCIATION, AND TRANSFIGURATION.

❡ *Upon the Feasts of the Purification, Annunciation, and Transfiguration.*

BECAUSE in the Mystery of the Word made flesh, thou hast caused a new light to shine in our hearts, to give the knowledge of thy glory in the face of thy Son Jesus Christ our Lord.

Therefore with Angels, etc.

EASTER.

¶ *Upon Easter Day, and seven days after.*

BUT chiefly are we bound to praise thee for the glorious Resurrection of thy Son Jesus Christ our Lord: for he is the very Paschal Lamb, which was offered for us, and hath taken away the sin of the world; who by his death hath destroyed death, and by his rising to life again hath restored to us everlasting life.

Therefore with Angels, etc.

ASCENSION.

¶ *Upon Ascension Day, and seven days after.*

THROUGH thy most dearly beloved Son Jesus Christ our Lord; who, after his most glorious Resurrection, manifestly appeared to all his Apostles, and in their sight ascended up into heaven, to prepare a place for us; that where he is, thither we might also ascend, and reign with him in glory.

Therefore with Angels, etc.

WHITSUNTIDE.

¶ *Upon Whitsunday, and six days after.*

THROUGH Jesus Christ our Lord; according to whose most true promise, the Holy Ghost came down as at this time from heaven, lighting upon the disciples, to teach them, and to lead them into all truth; giving them boldness with fervent zeal constantly to preach the Gospel unto all nations; whereby we have been brought out of darkness and error into the clear light and true knowledge of thee, and of thy Son Jesus Christ.

Therefore with Angels, etc.

TRINITY SUNDAY.

¶ *Upon the Feast of Trinity only.*

WHO, with thine only-begotten Son, and the Holy Ghost, art one God, one Lord, in Trinity of Persons and in Unity of Substance. For that which we believe of thy glory, O Father, the same we believe of the Son, and of the Holy Ghost, without any difference of inequality.

Therefore with Angels, etc.

¶ *Or this.*

FOR the precious death and merits of thy Son Jesus Christ our Lord, and for the sending to us of the Holy Ghost, the Comforter; who are one with thee in thy Eternal Godhead.

Therefore with Angels, etc.

ALL SAINTS.

¶ *Upon All Saints' Day, and seven days after.*

WHO, in the multitude of thy Saints, hast compassed us about with so great a cloud of witnesses that we, rejoicing in their fellowship, may run with patience the race that is set before us, and, together with them, may receive the crown of glory that fadeth not away.

Therefore with Angels and Archangels, and with all the company of heaven, we laud and magnify thy glorious Name; evermore praising thee, and saying,

HOLY, HOLY, HOLY, Lord God ¶ *Priest and People.* of hosts, Heaven and earth are full of thy glory: Glory be to thee, O Lord Most High. Amen.

Holy Communion

ALL glory be to thee, Almighty God, our heavenly Father, for that thou, of thy tender mercy, didst give thine only Son Jesus Christ to suffer death upon the Cross for our redemption; who made there (by his one oblation of himself once offered) a full, perfect, and sufficient sacrifice, oblation, and satisfaction, for the sins of the whole world; and did institute, and in his holy Gospel command us to continue, a perpetual memory of that his precious death and sacrifice, until his coming again: For in the night in which he was betrayed, (*a*) he took Bread; and when he had given thanks, (*b*) he brake it, and gave it to his disciples, saying, Take, eat, (*c*) this is my Body, which is given for you; Do this in remembrance of me. Likewise, after supper, (*d*) he took the Cup; and when he had given thanks, he gave it to them, saying, Drink ye all of this; for (*e*) this is my Blood of the New Testament, which is shed for you, and for many, for the remission of sins; Do this, as oft as ye shall drink it, in remembrance of me.

(*a*) *Here the Priest is to take the Paten into his hands.*

(*b*) *And here to break the Bread.*

(*c*) *And here to lay his hand upon all the Bread.*

(*d*) *Here he is to take the Cup into his hands.*

(*e*) *And here he is to lay his hand upon every vessel in which there is any Wine to be consecrated.*

WHEREFORE, O Lord and heavenly Father, according to the institution of thy dearly beloved Son our Saviour Jesus Christ, we, thy humble servants, do celebrate and make here before thy Divine Majesty, with these thy holy gifts, which we now offer unto thee, the memorial thy Son hath commanded

The Oblation.

The Consecration

The word "consecration" means to "make holy." The Prayer of Consecration continues our thanksgiving for all God's gifts. We remember together with thankful hearts how our Lord Jesus Christ lived with us, died for us, and promised to be with us always. With this thanksgiving, all of our gifts—our money, our bread and wine, our prayers, our selves—are offered to God. They are blessed by Him, and given back to us made new.

us to make; having in remembrance his blessed passion and precious death, his mighty resurrection and glorious ascension; rendering unto thee most hearty thanks for the innumerable benefits procured unto us by the same.

A*ND* we most humbly beseech thee, O merciful Father, to hear us; and, of *The Invocation.* thy almighty goodness, vouchsafe to bless and sanctify, with thy Word and Holy Spirit, these thy gifts and creatures of bread and wine; that we, receiving them according to thy Son our Saviour Jesus Christ's holy institution, in remembrance of his death and passion, may be partakers of his most blessed Body and Blood.

A*ND* we earnestly desire thy fatherly goodness, mercifully to accept this our sacrifice of praise and thanksgiving; most humbly beseeching thee to grant that, by the merits and death of thy Son Jesus Christ, and through faith in his blood, we, and all thy whole Church, may obtain remission of our sins, and all other benefits of his passion. And here we offer and present unto thee, O Lord, our selves, our souls and bodies, to be a reasonable, holy, and living sacrifice unto thee; humbly beseeching thee, that we, and all others who shall be partakers of this Holy Communion, may worthily receive the most precious Body and Blood of thy Son Jesus Christ, be filled with thy grace and heavenly benediction, and made one body with him, that he may dwell in us, and we in him. And although we are unworthy, through our manifold sins, to offer unto thee any sacrifice; yet we beseech thee to accept this our bounden duty and service; not weighing our merits, but pardoning our offences, through Jesus Christ our Lord; by whom, and with whom, in the unity of the Holy Ghost, all honour and glory be unto thee, O Father Almighty, world without end. *Amen.*

Holy Communion

And now, as our Saviour Christ hath taught us, we are bold to say,

OUR Father, who art in heaven, Hallowed be thy Name. Thy kingdom come. Thy will be done, On earth as it is in heaven. Give us this day our daily bread. And forgive us our trespasses, As we forgive those who trespass against us. And lead us not into temptation, But deliver us from evil. For thine is the kingdom, and the power, and the glory, for ever and ever. Amen.

¶ *Then shall the Priest, kneeling down at the Lord's Table, say, in the name of all those who shall receive the Communion, this Prayer following.*

WE do not presume to come to this thy Table, O merciful Lord, trusting in our own righteousness, but in thy manifold and great mercies. We are not worthy so much as to gather up the crumbs under thy Table. But thou art the same Lord, whose property is always to have mercy: Grant us therefore, gracious Lord, so to eat the flesh of thy dear Son Jesus Christ, and to drink his blood, that our sinful bodies may be made clean by his body, and our souls washed through his most precious blood, and that we may evermore dwell in him, and he in us. *Amen.*

¶ *Here may be sung a Hymn.*

¶ *Then shall the Priest and People receive the Holy Communion. And when he delivers the Bread, the Priest shall say,*

THE Body of our Lord Jesus Christ, which was given for thee, preserve thy body and soul unto everlasting life. Take and eat this in remembrance that Christ died for thee, and feed on him in thy heart by faith, with thanksgiving.

The Communion and Thanksgiving

After the Consecration, God gives Himself to the members of His family in the Sacrament. They go up to His table together to receive the blessed Bread and Wine for strength and refreshment as His children. This is what we call Communion.

After the Communion, we give thanks once more to God in prayer and in song. We are glad to be members of this family and to have God our Father with us wherever we go.

Holy Communion

⁋ And the Minister who delivers the Cup shall say,

THE Blood of our Lord Jesus Christ, which was shed for thee, preserve thy body and soul unto everlasting life. Drink this in remembrance that Christ's Blood was shed for thee, and be thankful.

⁋ If the consecrated Bread or Wine be spent before all have communi-cated, the Priest is to consecrate more, according to the Form before prescribed; beginning at, All glory be to thee, Almighty God, *and ending with these words,* partakers of his most blessed Body and Blood.

⁋ When all have communicated, the Priest shall return to the Lord's Table, and reverently place upon it what remaineth of the consecrated Elements, covering the same with a fair linen cloth.

⁋ Then shall the Priest say,

Let us pray.

ALMIGHTY and everliving God, we most heartily thank thee, for that thou dost vouchsafe to feed us who have duly received these holy mysteries, with the spiritual food of the most precious Body and Blood of thy Son our Sav-iour Jesus Christ; and dost assure us thereby of thy favour and goodness towards us; and that we are very members incorporate in the mystical body of thy Son, which is the blessed company of all faithful people; and are also heirs through hope of thy everlasting kingdom, by the merits of his most precious death and passion. And we humbly be-seech thee, O heavenly Father, so to assist us with thy grace, that we may continue in that holy fellowship, and do all such good works as thou hast prepared for us to walk in; through Jesus Christ our Lord, to whom, with thee and the Holy Ghost, be all honour and glory, world without end. *Amen.*

⁋ Then shall be said the Gloria in excelsis, all standing, or some proper Hymn.

Holy Communion

GLORY be to God on high, and on earth peace, good will towards men. We praise thee, we bless thee, we worship thee, we glorify thee, we give thanks to thee for thy great glory, O Lord God, heavenly King, God the Father Almighty.

O Lord, the only-begotten Son, Jesus Christ; O Lord God, Lamb of God, Son of the Father, that takest away the sins of the world, have mercy upon us. Thou that takest away the sins of the world, receive our prayer. Thou that sittest at the right hand of God the Father, have mercy upon us.

For thou only art holy; thou only art the Lord; thou only, O Christ, with the Holy Ghost, art most high in the glory of God the Father. Amen.

¶ *Then, the People kneeling, the Priest (the Bishop if he be present) shall let them depart with this Blessing.*

THE Peace of God, which passeth all understanding, keep your hearts and minds in the knowledge and love of God, and of his Son Jesus Christ our Lord: And the Blessing of God Almighty, the Father, the Son, and the Holy Ghost, be amongst you, and remain with you always. *Amen.*

Notes on

The Church Year

with

The Collects

To Be Used

Throughout the Year

The Church Year

We all hang calendars in our homes to remind us what day it is and to help us remember the days and times when we have important things to do or special places to go. The Church also has a calendar reminding us of Jesus, our Lord, and of His Saints. It tells us of the special days when we are to meet together for worship.

The seasons spring, summer, fall, and winter are familiar to all of us. The Church has seasons, too. In the Church Year the seasons are Advent, Christmastide, Epiphany, Pre-Lent, Lent, Eastertide, Ascensiontide, Whitsuntide, and Trinity. As we follow the Church Year in our worship, we hear the story of God's love for us and for all people.

In the rest of this book you can read about the Church seasons. You can also find the prayers to be read in church on each Sunday and special day in the year. The Book of Common Prayer has the Epistles and Gospels for these days, also.

Notes on the Church Year
and
The Collects

Advent Season

The word "advent" means "coming." In the Advent Season we prepare for the coming of our Lord at Christmas. We do this in several ways. First, we prepare our hearts to receive Him. Just as we look forward with joy to the coming of a guest to our home, so we await with longing and love the coming of Christ among us. We also prepare for His coming by thinking of others instead of ourselves. One way we can show our love for others is to make gifts for them. In the four weeks of Advent we spend many hours preparing the gifts we will give our family and friends at Christmas.

✝

The First Sunday in Advent.

ALMIGHTY God, give us grace that we may cast away the works of darkness, and put upon us the armour of light, now in the time of this mortal life, in which thy Son Jesus Christ came to visit us in great humility; that in the last day, when he shall come again in his glorious majesty to judge both the quick and the dead, we may rise to the life immortal, through him who liveth and reigneth with thee and the Holy Ghost, now and ever. *Amen.*

❡ *This Collect is to be repeated every day, after the other Collects in Advent, until Christmas Day.*

The Second Sunday in Advent.

BLESSED Lord, who hast caused all holy Scriptures to be written for our learning; Grant that we may in such wise hear them, read, mark, learn, and inwardly digest them, that by patience and comfort of thy holy Word, we may embrace, and ever hold fast, the blessed hope of everlasting life, which thou hast given us in our Saviour Jesus Christ. *Amen.*

The Church Year

The Third Sunday in Advent.

O LORD Jesus Christ, who at thy first coming didst send thy messenger to prepare thy way before thee; Grant that the ministers and stewards of thy mysteries may likewise so prepare and make ready thy way, by turning the hearts of the disobedient to the wisdom of the just, that at thy second coming to judge the world we may be found an acceptable people in thy sight, who livest and reignest with the Father and the Holy Spirit ever, one God, world without end. *Amen.*

The Fourth Sunday in Advent.

O LORD, raise up, we pray thee, thy power, and come among us, and with great might succour us; that whereas, through our sins and wickedness, we are sore let and hindered in running the race that is set before us, thy bountiful grace and mercy may speedily help and deliver us; through Jesus Christ our Lord, to whom, with thee and the Holy Ghost, be honour and glory, world without end. *Amen.*

Christmastide

Christmas Day is the birthday of our Lord Jesus Christ. On this day Christians everywhere joyfully remember that the Son of God came among us to show forth God's love. No one thought that the great Son of God would come into the world as a baby, but that is how Christ came.

At Christmas time we give presents to our family and friends. We also prepare gifts for many other persons throughout the world. This is our way of giving birthday presents to our Lord. Christmas is a time of rejoicing, for Jesus Christ loves all people everywhere. He came into the world to give Himself for all of us.

✝

The Nativity of our Lord, or the Birthday of Christ,
commonly called Christmas Day.
[December 25.]

ALMIGHTY God, who hast given us thy only-begotten Son to take our nature upon him, and as at this time to be born of a pure virgin; Grant that we being regenerate, and made thy children by adoption and grace, may daily be renewed by thy Holy Spirit; through the same our Lord Jesus Christ, who liveth and reigneth with thee and the same Spirit ever, one God, world without end. *Amen.*

❡ *This Collect is to be said daily throughout the Octave.*

O GOD, who makest us glad with the yearly remembrance of the birth of thine only Son Jesus Christ; Grant that as we joyfully receive him for our Redeemer, so we may with sure confidence behold him when he shall

come to be our Judge, who liveth and reigneth with thee and the Holy Ghost, one God, world without end. *Amen.*

Saint Stephen, Deacon and Martyr.
[*December 26.*]

GRANT, O Lord, that, in all our sufferings here upon earth for the testimony of thy truth, we may stedfastly look up to heaven, and by faith behold the glory that shall be revealed; and, being filled with the Holy Ghost, may learn to love and bless our persecutors by the example of thy first Martyr Saint Stephen, who prayed for his murderers to thee, O blessed Jesus, who standest at the right hand of God to succour all those who suffer for thee, our only Mediator and Advocate. *Amen.*

Saint John, Apostle and Evangelist.
[*December 27.*]

MERCIFUL Lord, we beseech thee to cast thy bright beams of light upon thy Church, that it, being illumined by the doctrine of thy blessed Apostle and Evangelist Saint John, may so walk in the light of thy truth, that it may at length attain to life everlasting; through Jesus Christ our Lord. *Amen.*

The Holy Innocents.
[*December 28.*]

O ALMIGHTY God, who out of the mouths of babes and sucklings hast ordained strength, and madest infants to glorify thee by their deaths; Mortify and kill all vices in us, and so strengthen us by thy grace, that by the innocency of our lives, and constancy of our faith even unto death, we may glorify thy holy Name; through Jesus Christ our Lord. *Amen.*

The Church Year

The First Sunday after Christmas Day.

ALMIGHTY God, who hast given us thy only-begotten Son to take our nature upon him, and as at this time to be born of a pure virgin; Grant that we being regenerate, and made thy children by adoption and grace, may daily be renewed by thy Holy Spirit; through the same our Lord Jesus Christ, who liveth and reigneth with thee and the same Spirit ever, one God, world without end. *Amen.*

The Circumcision of Christ.
[January 1.]

ALMIGHTY God, who madest thy blessed Son to be circumcised, and obedient to the law for man; Grant us the true circumcision of the Spirit; that, our hearts, and all our members, being mortified from all worldly and carnal lusts, we may in all things obey thy blessed will; through the same thy Son Jesus Christ our Lord. *Amen.*

The Second Sunday after Christmas Day.

ALMIGHTY God, who hast poured upon us the new light of thine incarnate Word; Grant that the same light enkindled in our hearts may shine forth in our lives; through Jesus Christ our Lord. *Amen.*

Epiphany Season

The Epiphany comes twelve days after Christmas Day. In a way it continues the Christmas celebration. On this day we celebrate the visit of the Wise Men to the Christ Child in Bethlehem. The Wise Men represent all the many peoples of the world, of every land and race. Throughout the Epiphany Season we think especially of all these people for whom Christ came to show God's love.

✝

The Epiphany, or the Manifestation of Christ to the Gentiles.
[January 6.]

O GOD, who by the leading of a star didst manifest thy only-begotten Son to the Gentiles; Mercifully grant that we, who know thee now by faith, may after this life have the fruition of thy glorious Godhead; through the same thy Son Jesus Christ our Lord. *Amen.*

❡ *This Collect is to be said daily throughout the Octave.*

The First Sunday after the Epiphany.

O LORD, we beseech thee mercifully to receive the prayers of thy people who call upon thee; and grant that they may both perceive and know what things they ought to do, and also may have grace and power faithfully to fulfil the same; through Jesus Christ our Lord. *Amen.*

The Church Year

The Second Sunday after the Epiphany.

ALMIGHTY and everlasting God, who dost govern all things in heaven and earth; Mercifully hear the supplications of thy people, and grant us thy peace all the days of our life; through Jesus Christ our Lord. *Amen.*

The Third Sunday after the Epiphany.

ALMIGHTY and everlasting God, mercifully look upon our infirmities, and in all our dangers and necessities stretch forth thy right hand to help and defend us; through Jesus Christ our Lord. *Amen.*

The Fourth Sunday after the Epiphany.

O GOD, who knowest us to be set in the midst of so many and great dangers, that by reason of the frailty of our nature we cannot always stand upright; Grant to us such strength and protection, as may support us in all dangers, and carry us through all temptations; through Jesus Christ our Lord. *Amen.*

The Fifth Sunday after the Epiphany.

O LORD, we beseech thee to keep thy Church and household continually in thy true religion; that they who do lean only upon the hope of thy heavenly grace may evermore be defended by thy mighty power; through Jesus Christ our Lord. *Amen.*

The Church Year

The Sixth Sunday after the Epiphany.

O GOD, whose blessed Son was manifested that he might destroy the works of the devil, and make us the sons of God, and heirs of eternal life; Grant us, we beseech thee, that, having this hope, we may purify ourselves, even as he is pure; that, when he shall appear again with power and great glory, we may be made like unto him in his eternal and glorious kingdom; where with thee, O Father, and thee, O Holy Ghost, he liveth and reigneth ever, one God, world without end. *Amen.*

Pre-Lenten Season

After the Epiphany Season, the Church spends three weeks making ready for Lent. We call this season Pre-Lent. The Sundays in Pre-Lent have long Latin names. What the names say is that these Sundays are about seventy, sixty, and fifty days before Easter.

The Pre-Lenten Season gives us the time to plan how we are going to observe Lent. If we have not made a missionary offering during the Epiphany Season, now is a good time to make plans to do so during Lent.

✝

The Sunday called Septuagesima, or the third Sunday before Lent.

O LORD, we beseech thee favourably to hear the prayers of thy people; that we, who are justly punished for our offences, may be mercifully delivered by thy goodness, for the glory of thy Name; through Jesus Christ our Saviour, who liveth and reigneth with thee and the Holy Ghost ever, one God, world without end. *Amen.*

The Sunday called Sexagesima, or the second Sunday before Lent.

O LORD God, who seest that we put not our trust in any thing that we do; Mercifully grant that by thy power we may be defended against all adversity; through Jesus Christ our Lord. *Amen.*

The Church Year

The Sunday called Quinquagesima, or the
Sunday next before Lent.

O LORD, who hast taught us that all our doings without charity are nothing worth; Send thy Holy Ghost, and pour into our hearts that most excellent gift of charity, the very bond of peace and of all virtues, without which whosoever liveth is counted dead before thee. Grant this for thine only Son Jesus Christ's sake. *Amen.*

Lenten Season

Lent is the season in the Church Year when all who follow Jesus Christ remember especially how He suffered for our sake. Lent lasts for forty days because Jesus stayed forty days in the wilderness, fasting, praying, and preparing Himself for the work that God had given Him to do. In Lent, Jesus' followers fast and pray, too. To fast is to give up something we like very much. Fasting makes our wills stronger. It can also be a way of saving money to help others.

The first day of Lent is called Ash Wednesday. The last week in Lent is called Holy Week. During Holy Week we remember Jesus' last week on earth. On Thursday night He shared the Last Supper with His disciples. This was the first service of Holy Communion. On Good Friday Jesus suffered and died on the Cross for the sins of all the world.

*The first day of Lent, commonly called
Ash Wednesday.*

ALMIGHTY and everlasting God, who hatest nothing that thou hast made, and dost forgive the sins of all those who are penitent; Create and make in us new and contrite hearts, that we, worthily lamenting our sins and acknowledging our wretchedness, may obtain of thee, the God of all mercy, perfect remission and forgiveness; through Jesus Christ our Lord. *Amen.*

¶ *This Collect is to be said every day in Lent, after the Collect appointed for the day, until Palm Sunday.*

The Church Year

The First Sunday in Lent.

O LORD, who for our sake didst fast forty days and forty nights; Give us grace to use such abstinence, that, our flesh being subdued to the Spirit, we may ever obey thy godly motions in righteousness, and true holiness, to thy honour and glory, who livest and reignest with the Father and the Holy Ghost, one God, world without end. *Amen.*

The Second Sunday in Lent.

A LMIGHTY God, who seest that we have no power of ourselves to help ourselves; Keep us both outwardly in our bodies, and inwardly in our souls; that we may be defended from all adversities which may happen to the body, and from all evil thoughts which may assault and hurt the soul; through Jesus Christ our Lord. *Amen.*

The Third Sunday in Lent.

W E beseech thee, Almighty God, look upon the hearty desires of thy humble servants, and stretch forth the right hand of thy Majesty, to be our defence against all our enemies; through Jesus Christ our Lord. *Amen.*

The Fourth Sunday in Lent.

G RANT, we beseech thee, Almighty God, that we, who for our evil deeds do worthily deserve to be punished, by the comfort of thy grace may mercifully be relieved; through our Lord and Saviour Jesus Christ. *Amen.*

The Fifth Sunday in Lent, commonly called Passion Sunday.

W E beseech thee, Almighty God, mercifully to look upon thy people; that by thy great goodness they

may be governed and preserved evermore, both in body and soul; through Jesus Christ our Lord. *Amen.*

The Sunday next before Easter, commonly called Palm Sunday.

ALMIGHTY and everlasting God, who, of thy tender love towards mankind, hast sent thy Son, our Saviour Jesus Christ, to take upon him our flesh, and to suffer death upon the cross, that all mankind should follow the example of his great humility; Mercifully grant, that we may both follow the example of his patience, and also be made partakers of his resurrection; through the same Jesus Christ our Lord. *Amen.*

❡ *This Collect is to be said every day, after the Collect appointed for the day, until Good Friday.*

Monday before Easter.

ALMIGHTY God, whose most dear Son went not up to joy but first he suffered pain, and entered not into glory before he was crucified; Mercifully grant that we, walking in the way of the cross, may find it none other than the way of life and peace; through the same thy Son Jesus Christ our Lord. *Amen.*

Tuesday before Easter.

O LORD God, whose blessed Son, our Saviour, gave his back to the smiters and hid not his face from shame; Grant us grace to take joyfully the sufferings of the present time, in full assurance of the glory that shall be revealed; through the same thy Son Jesus Christ our Lord. *Amen.*

[83]

The Church Year

Wednesday before Easter.

ASSIST us mercifully with thy help, O Lord God of our salvation; that we may enter with joy upon the meditation of those mighty acts, whereby thou hast given unto us life and immortality; through Jesus Christ our Lord. *Amen.*

Thursday before Easter, commonly called
Maundy Thursday.

ALMIGHTY Father, whose dear Son, on the night before he suffered, did institute the Sacrament of his Body and Blood; Mercifully grant that we may thankfully receive the same in remembrance of him, who in these holy mysteries giveth us a pledge of life eternal; the same thy Son Jesus Christ our Lord, who now liveth and reigneth with thee and the Holy Spirit ever, one God, world without end. *Amen.*

Good Friday.

ALMIGHTY God, we beseech thee graciously to behold this thy family, for which our Lord Jesus Christ was contented to be betrayed, and given up into the hands of wicked men, and to suffer death upon the cross; who now liveth and reigneth with thee and the Holy Ghost ever, one God, world without end. *Amen.*

ALMIGHTY and everlasting God, by whose Spirit the whole body of the Church is governed and sanctified; Receive our supplications and prayers, which we offer before thee for all estates of men in thy holy Church, that every member of the same, in his vocation and ministry, may truly and godly serve thee; through our Lord and Saviour Jesus Christ. *Amen.*

[84]

The Church Year

Good Friday.

O MERCIFUL God, who hast made all men, and hatest nothing that thou hast made, nor desirest the death of a sinner, but rather that he should be converted and live; Have mercy upon all who know thee not as thou art revealed in the Gospel of thy Son. Take from them all ignorance, hardness of heart, and contempt of thy Word; and so fetch them home, blessed Lord, to thy fold, that they may be made one flock under one shepherd, Jesus Christ our Lord, who liveth and reigneth with thee and the Holy Spirit, one God, world without end. *Amen.*

Easter Even.

G RANT, O Lord, that as we are baptized into the death of thy blessed Son, our Saviour Jesus Christ, so by continual mortifying our corrupt affections we may be buried with him; and that through the grave, and gate of death, we may pass to our joyful resurrection; for his merits, who died, and was buried, and rose again for us, the same thy Son Jesus Christ our Lord. *Amen.*

Eastertide

The Son of God, born a babe in Bethlehem, grew to be a man who lived among the people of Palestine and loved and taught them. He suffered and died on the Cross for the sins of all mankind. On the third day God raised Him from the dead. We call the day of His resurrection Easter. In Eastertide the Church celebrates the resurrection of our Lord and rejoices at this great and wonderful act of God. The resurrection of the Lord Jesus shows us always that we are able by His help to overcome temptation and sin. It tells us, too, that we need never be afraid to die or afraid when someone we love dies.

Easter Day.

ALMIGHTY God, who through thine only-begotten Son Jesus Christ hast overcome death, and opened unto us the gate of everlasting life; We humbly beseech thee that, as by thy special grace preventing us thou dost put into our minds good desires, so by thy continual help we may bring the same to good effect; through the same Jesus Christ our Lord, who liveth and reigneth with thee and the Holy Ghost ever, one God, world without end. *Amen.*

❡ *This Collect is to be said daily throughout Easter Week.*

O GOD, who for our redemption didst give thine only-begotten Son to the death of the Cross, and by his glorious resurrection hast delivered us from the power of our enemy; Grant us so to die daily from sin, that we may

[86]

evermore live with him in the joy of his resurrection; through the same thy Son Christ our Lord. *Amen.*

Monday in Easter Week.

O GOD, whose blessed Son did manifest himself to his disciples in the breaking of bread; Open, we pray thee, the eyes of our faith, that we may behold thee in all thy works; through the same thy Son Jesus Christ our Lord. *Amen.*

Tuesday in Easter Week.

GRANT, we beseech thee, Almighty God, that we who celebrate with reverence the Paschal feast, may be found worthy to attain to everlasting joys; through Jesus Christ our Lord. *Amen.*

The First Sunday after Easter.

ALMIGHTY Father, who hast given thine only Son to die for our sins, and to rise again for our justification; Grant us so to put away the leaven of malice and wickedness, that we may always serve thee in pureness of living and truth; through the merits of the same thy Son Jesus Christ our Lord. *Amen.*

The Second Sunday after Easter.

ALMIGHTY God, who hast given thine only Son to be unto us both a sacrifice for sin, and also an ensample of godly life; Give us grace that we may always most thankfully receive that his inestimable benefit, and also daily endeavour ourselves to follow the blessed steps of his most holy life; through the same thy Son Jesus Christ our Lord. *Amen.*

The Church Year

The Third Sunday after Easter.

ALMIGHTY God, who showest to them that are in error the light of thy truth, to the intent that they may return into the way of righteousness; Grant unto all those who are admitted into the fellowship of Christ's Religion, that they may avoid those things that are contrary to their profession, and follow all such things as are agreeable to the same; through our Lord Jesus Christ. *Amen.*

The Fourth Sunday after Easter.

O ALMIGHTY God, who alone canst order the unruly wills and affections of sinful men; Grant unto thy people, that they may love the thing which thou commandest, and desire that which thou dost promise; that so, among the sundry and manifold changes of the world, our hearts may surely there be fixed, where true joys are to be found; through Jesus Christ our Lord. *Amen.*

The Fifth Sunday after Easter, commonly called Rogation Sunday.

O LORD, from whom all good things do come; Grant to us thy humble servants, that by thy holy inspiration we may think those things that are good, and by thy merciful guiding may perform the same; through our Lord Jesus Christ. *Amen.*

Ascensiontide

Forty days after our Lord's resurrection, He ascended to the Father in heaven. We call that day Ascension Day. The ascension of Jesus Christ means that He is Lord of all our life. He is the King who rules forever.

✝

The Ascension Day.

GRANT, we beseech thee, Almighty God, that like as we do believe thy only-begotten Son our Lord Jesus Christ to have ascended into the heavens; so we may also in heart and mind thither ascend, and with him continually dwell, who liveth and reigneth with thee and the Holy Ghost, one God, world without end. *Amen.*

❡ *This Collect is to be said daily throughout the Octave.*

The Sunday after Ascension Day.

O GOD, the King of glory, who hast exalted thine only Son Jesus Christ with great triumph unto thy kingdom in heaven; We beseech thee, leave us not comfortless; but send to us thine Holy Ghost to comfort us, and exalt us unto the same place whither our Saviour Christ is gone before, who liveth and reigneth with thee and the same Holy Ghost, one God, world without end. *Amen.*

Whitsuntide

God came anew to the followers of Jesus Christ in the Person of the Holy Spirit. He did this so that they might have power to go out to preach and teach in the Name of Jesus Christ. God's Spirit is always with His Church, ready to gather His people together in unity.

We remember on a special day that God came among us and continues to come among us in the Person of the Holy Spirit. We call this day Whitsunday. We also call it Pentecost.

✝

Pentecost, commonly called Whitsunday.

O GOD, who as at this time didst teach the hearts of thy faithful people, by sending to them the light of thy Holy Spirit; Grant us by the same Spirit to have a right judgment in all things, and evermore to rejoice in his holy comfort; through the merits of Christ Jesus our Saviour, who liveth and reigneth with thee, in the unity of the same Spirit, one God, world without end. *Amen.*

❡ *This Collect is to be said daily throughout Whitsun Week.*

ALMIGHTY and most merciful God, grant, we beseech thee, that by the indwelling of thy Holy Spirit, we may be enlightened and strengthened for thy service; through Jesus Christ our Lord, who liveth and reigneth with thee in the unity of the same Spirit ever, one God, world without end. *Amen.*

The Church Year

Monday in Whitsun Week.

SEND, we beseech thee, Almighty God, thy Holy Spirit into our hearts, that he may direct and rule us according to thy will, comfort us in all our afflictions, defend us from all error, and lead us into all truth; through Jesus Christ our Lord, who with thee and the same Holy Spirit liveth and reigneth, one God, world without end. *Amen.*

Tuesday in Whitsun Week.

GRANT, we beseech thee, merciful God, that thy Church, being gathered together in unity by thy Holy Spirit, may manifest thy power among all peoples, to the glory of thy Name; through Jesus Christ our Lord, who liveth and reigneth with thee and the same Spirit, one God, world without end. *Amen.*

Trinity Season

Trinity Sunday is the first day of the Trinity Season. It is a day on which the Church praises God—Father, Son, and Holy Spirit—who is one God, now and forever.

The Trinity Season lasts almost half the Church Year. It gives us time to see that we can grow in many ways as we worship and obey God the Father, love and follow God the Son, and let the Holy Spirit come into our lives. The Epistles and Gospels for the Trinity Season are almost always about the teaching of Christ.

✝

Trinity Sunday.

ALMIGHTY and everlasting God, who hast given unto us thy servants grace, by the confession of a true faith, to acknowledge the glory of the eternal Trinity, and in the power of the Divine Majesty to worship the Unity; We beseech thee that thou wouldest keep us stedfast in this faith, and evermore defend us from all adversities, who livest and reignest, one God, world without end. *Amen.*

The First Sunday after Trinity.

O GOD, the strength of all those who put their trust in thee; Mercifully accept our prayers; and because, through the weakness of our mortal nature, we can do no good thing without thee, grant us the help of thy grace, that in keeping thy commandments we may please thee, both in will and deed; through Jesus Christ our Lord. *Amen.*

The Church Year

The Second Sunday after Trinity.

O LORD, who never failest to help and govern those whom thou dost bring up in thy stedfast fear and love; Keep us, we beseech thee, under the protection of thy good providence, and make us to have a perpetual fear and love of thy holy Name; through Jesus Christ our Lord. *Amen.*

The Third Sunday after Trinity.

O LORD, we beseech thee mercifully to hear us; and grant that we, to whom thou hast given an hearty desire to pray, may, by thy mighty aid, be defended and comforted in all dangers and adversities; through Jesus Christ our Lord. *Amen.*

The Fourth Sunday after Trinity.

O GOD, the protector of all that trust in thee, without whom nothing is strong, nothing is holy; Increase and multiply upon us thy mercy; that, thou being our ruler and guide, we may so pass through things temporal, that we finally lose not the things eternal. Grant this, O heavenly Father, for the sake of Jesus Christ our Lord. *Amen.*

The Fifth Sunday after Trinity.

GRANT, O Lord, we beseech thee, that the course of this world may be so peaceably ordered by thy governance, that thy Church may joyfully serve thee in all godly quietness; through Jesus Christ our Lord. *Amen.*

The Sixth Sunday after Trinity.

O GOD, who hast prepared for those who love thee such good things as pass man's understanding; Pour into our hearts such love toward thee, that we, loving thee

[95]

above all things, may obtain thy promises, which exceed all that we can desire; through Jesus Christ our Lord. *Amen.*

The Seventh Sunday after Trinity.

LORD of all power and might, who art the author and giver of all good things; Graft in our hearts the love of thy Name, increase in us true religion, nourish us with all goodness, and of thy great mercy keep us in the same; through Jesus Christ our Lord. *Amen.*

The Eighth Sunday after Trinity.

O GOD, whose never-failing providence ordereth all things both in heaven and earth; We humbly beseech thee to put away from us all hurtful things, and to give us those things which are profitable for us; through Jesus Christ our Lord. *Amen.*

The Ninth Sunday after Trinity.

GRANT to us, Lord, we beseech thee, the spirit to think and do always such things as are right; that we, who cannot do any thing that is good without thee, may by thee be enabled to live according to thy will; through Jesus Christ our Lord. *Amen.*

The Tenth Sunday after Trinity.

LET thy merciful ears, O Lord, be open to the prayers of thy humble servants; and, that they may obtain their petitions, make them to ask such things as shall please thee; through Jesus Christ our Lord. *Amen.*

The Eleventh Sunday after Trinity.

O GOD, who declarest thy almighty power chiefly in showing mercy and pity; Mercifully grant unto us such a measure of thy grace, that we, running the way of thy commandments, may obtain thy gracious promises, and be made partakers of thy heavenly treasure; through Jesus Christ our Lord. *Amen.*

The Twelfth Sunday after Trinity.

ALMIGHTY and everlasting God, who art always more ready to hear than we to pray, and art wont to give more than either we desire or deserve; Pour down upon us the abundance of thy mercy; forgiving us those things whereof our conscience is afraid, and giving us those good things which we are not worthy to ask, but through the merits and mediation of Jesus Christ, thy Son, our Lord. *Amen.*

The Thirteenth Sunday after Trinity.

ALMIGHTY and merciful God, of whose only gift it cometh that thy faithful people do unto thee true and laudable service; Grant, we beseech thee, that we may so faithfully serve thee in this life, that we fail not finally to attain thy heavenly promises; through the merits of Jesus Christ our Lord. *Amen.*

The Fourteenth Sunday after Trinity.

ALMIGHTY and everlasting God, give unto us the increase of faith, hope, and charity; and, that we may obtain that which thou dost promise, make us to love that which thou dost command; through Jesus Christ our Lord. *Amen.*

The Fifteenth Sunday after Trinity.

KEEP, we beseech thee, O Lord, thy Church with thy perpetual mercy; and, because the frailty of man without thee cannot but fall, keep us ever by thy help from all things hurtful, and lead us to all things profitable to our salvation; through Jesus Christ our Lord. *Amen.*

The Sixteenth Sunday after Trinity.

O LORD, we beseech thee, let thy continual pity cleanse and defend thy Church; and, because it cannot continue in safety without thy succour, preserve it evermore by thy help and goodness; through Jesus Christ our Lord. *Amen.*

The Seventeenth Sunday after Trinity.

LORD, we pray thee that thy grace may always prevent and follow us, and make us continually to be given to all good works; through Jesus Christ our Lord. *Amen.*

The Eighteenth Sunday after Trinity.

LORD, we beseech thee, grant thy people grace to withstand the temptations of the world, the flesh, and the devil; and with pure hearts and minds to follow thee, the only God; through Jesus Christ our Lord. *Amen.*

The Nineteenth Sunday after Trinity.

O GOD, forasmuch as without thee we are not able to please thee; Mercifully grant that thy Holy Spirit may in all things direct and rule our hearts; through Jesus Christ our Lord. *Amen.*

The Twentieth Sunday after Trinity.

O ALMIGHTY and most merciful God, of thy bountiful goodness keep us, we beseech thee, from all things that may hurt us; that we, being ready both in body and soul, may cheerfully accomplish those things which thou commandest; through Jesus Christ our Lord. *Amen.*

The Church Year

The Twenty-first Sunday after Trinity.

GRANT, we beseech thee, merciful Lord, to thy faithful people pardon and peace, that they may be cleansed from all their sins, and serve thee with a quiet mind; through Jesus Christ our Lord. *Amen.*

The Twenty-second Sunday after Trinity.

LORD, we beseech thee to keep thy household the Church in continual godliness; that through thy protection it may be free from all adversities, and devoutly given to serve thee in good works, to the glory of thy Name; through Jesus Christ our Lord. *Amen.*

The Twenty-third Sunday after Trinity.

O GOD, our refuge and strength, who art the author of all godliness; Be ready, we beseech thee, to hear the devout prayers of thy Church; and grant that those things which we ask faithfully we may obtain effectually; through Jesus Christ our Lord. *Amen.*

The Twenty-fourth Sunday after Trinity.

O LORD, we beseech thee, absolve thy people from their offences; that through thy bountiful goodness we may all be delivered from the bands of those sins, which by our frailty we have committed. Grant this, O heavenly Father, for the sake of Jesus Christ, our blessed Lord and Saviour. *Amen.*

The Sunday next before Advent.

STIR up, we beseech thee, O Lord, the wills of thy faithful people; that they, plenteously bringing forth the fruit of good works, may by thee be plenteously rewarded; through Jesus Christ our Lord. *Amen.*

Holy Days

Saint Andrew the Apostle.
[*November 30.*]

ALMIGHTY God, who didst give such grace unto thy holy Apostle Saint Andrew, that he readily obeyed the calling of thy Son Jesus Christ, and followed him without delay; Grant unto us all, that we, being called by thy holy Word, may forthwith give up ourselves obediently to fulfil thy holy commandments; through the same Jesus Christ our Lord. *Amen.*

Saint Thomas the Apostle.
[*December 21.*]

ALMIGHTY and everliving God, who, for the greater confirmation of the faith, didst suffer thy holy Apostle Thomas to be doubtful in thy Son's resurrection; Grant us so perfectly, and without all doubt, to believe in thy Son Jesus Christ, that our faith in thy sight may never be reproved. Hear us, O Lord, through the same Jesus Christ, to whom, with thee and the Holy Ghost, be all honour and glory, now and for evermore. *Amen.*

The Conversion of Saint Paul.
[*January 25.*]

O GOD, who, through the preaching of the blessed Apostle Saint Paul, hast caused the light of the Gospel to shine throughout the world; Grant, we beseech thee, that we, having his wonderful conversion in remembrance, may show forth our thankfulness unto thee for the same, by following the holy doctrine which he taught; through Jesus Christ our Lord. *Amen.*

The Church Year

The Presentation of Christ in the Temple,
commonly called
The Purification of Saint Mary the Virgin.
[*February 2.*]

ALMIGHTY and everliving God, we humbly beseech thy Majesty, that, as thy only-begotten Son was this day presented in the temple in substance of our flesh, so we may be presented unto thee with pure and clean hearts, by the same thy Son Jesus Christ our Lord. *Amen.*

Saint Matthias the Apostle.
[*February 24.*]

O ALMIGHTY God, who into the place of the traitor Judas didst choose thy faithful servant Matthias to be of the number of the twelve Apostles; Grant that thy Church, being alway preserved from false Apostles, may be ordered and guided by faithful and true pastors; through Jesus Christ our Lord. *Amen.*

The Annunciation of the blessed Virgin Mary.
[*March 25.*]

WE beseech thee, O Lord, pour thy grace into our hearts; that, as we have known the incarnation of thy Son Jesus Christ by the message of an angel, so by his cross and passion we may be brought unto the glory of his resurrection; through the same Jesus Christ our Lord. *Amen.*

Saint Mark the Evangelist.
[*April 25.*]

O ALMIGHTY God, who hast instructed thy holy Church with the heavenly doctrine of thy Evangelist Saint Mark; Give us grace that, being not like children carried away with every blast of vain doctrine, we may be established in the truth of thy holy Gospel; through Jesus Christ our Lord. *Amen.*

Saint Philip and Saint James, Apostles.
[May 1.]

O ALMIGHTY God, whom truly to know is everlasting life; Grant us perfectly to know thy Son Jesus Christ to be the way, the truth, and the life; that, following the steps of thy holy Apostles, Saint Philip and Saint James, we may stedfastly walk in the way that leadeth to eternal life; through the same thy Son Jesus Christ our Lord. *Amen.*

Saint Barnabas the Apostle.
[June 11.]

O LORD God Almighty, who didst endue thy holy Apostle Barnabas with singular gifts of the Holy Ghost; Leave us not, we beseech thee, destitute of thy manifold gifts, nor yet of grace to use them alway to thy honour and glory; through Jesus Christ our Lord. *Amen.*

Saint John Baptist.
[June 24.]

ALMIGHTY God, by whose providence thy servant John Baptist was wonderfully born, and sent to prepare the way of thy Son our Saviour by preaching repentance; Make us so to follow his doctrine and holy life, that we may truly repent according to his preaching; and after his example constantly speak the truth, boldly rebuke vice, and patiently suffer for the truth's sake; through the same thy Son Jesus Christ our Lord. *Amen.*

The Church Year

Saint Peter the Apostle.
[June 29.]

O ALMIGHTY God, who by thy Son Jesus Christ didst give to thy Apostle Saint Peter many excellent gifts, and commandedst him earnestly to feed thy flock; Make, we beseech thee, all Bishops and Pastors diligently to preach thy holy Word, and the people obediently to follow the same, that they may receive the crown of everlasting glory; through the same thy Son Jesus Christ our Lord. *Amen.*

Saint James the Apostle.
[July 25.]

GRANT, O merciful God, that, as thine holy Apostle Saint James, leaving his father and all that he had, without delay was obedient unto the calling of thy Son Jesus Christ, and followed him; so we, forsaking all worldly and carnal affections, may be evermore ready to follow thy holy commandments; through the same Jesus Christ our Lord. *Amen.*

The Transfiguration of Christ.
[August 6.]

O GOD, who on the mount didst reveal to chosen witnesses thine only-begotten Son wonderfully transfigured, in raiment white and glistering; Mercifully grant that we, being delivered from the disquietude of this world, may be permitted to behold the King in his beauty, who with thee, O Father, and thee, O Holy Ghost, liveth and reigneth, one God, world without end. *Amen.*

Saint Bartholomew the Apostle.
[August 24.]

O ALMIGHTY and everlasting God, who didst give to thine Apostle Bartholomew grace truly to believe and to preach thy Word; Grant, we beseech thee, unto thy Church, to love that Word which he believed, and both to preach and receive the same; through Jesus Christ our Lord. *Amen.*

Saint Matthew, Apostle and Evangelist.
[September 21.]

O ALMIGHTY God, who by thy blessed Son didst call Matthew from the receipt of custom to be an Apostle and Evangelist; Grant us grace to forsake all covetous desires, and inordinate love of riches, and to follow the same thy Son Jesus Christ, who liveth and reigneth with thee and the Holy Ghost, one God, world without end. *Amen.*

Saint Michael and all Angels.
[September 29.]

O EVERLASTING God, who hast ordained and constituted the services of Angels and men in a wonderful order; Mercifully grant that, as thy holy Angels always do thee service in heaven, so, by thy appointment, they may succour and defend us on earth; through Jesus Christ our Lord. *Amen.*

Saint Luke the Evangelist.
[October 18.]

ALMIGHTY God, who didst inspire thy servant Saint Luke the Physician, to set forth in the Gospel the love and healing power of thy Son; Manifest in thy Church the like power and love, to the healing of our bodies and our souls; through the same thy Son Jesus Christ our Lord. *Amen.*

The Church Year

Saint Simon and Saint Jude, Apostles.
[October 28.]

O ALMIGHTY God, who hast built thy Church upon the foundation of the Apostles and Prophets, Jesus Christ himself being the head corner-stone; Grant us so to be joined together in unity of spirit by their doctrine, that we may be made an holy temple acceptable unto thee; through the same Jesus Christ our Lord. *Amen.*

All Saints' Day.
[November 1.]

O ALMIGHTY God, who hast knit together thine elect in one communion and fellowship, in the mystical body of thy Son Christ our Lord; Grant us grace so to follow thy blessed Saints in all virtuous and godly living, that we may come to those unspeakable joys which thou hast prepared for those who unfeignedly love thee; through the same thy Son Jesus Christ our Lord. *Amen.*

❡ *This Collect is to be said daily throughout the Octave.*

A Saint's Day.

ALMIGHTY and everlasting God, who dost enkindle the flame of thy love in the hearts of the Saints; Grant to us, thy humble servants, the same faith and power of love; that, as we rejoice in their triumphs, we may profit by their examples; through Jesus Christ our Lord. *Amen.*

❡ *Or this.*

O ALMIGHTY God, who hast called us to faith in thee, and hast compassed us about with so great a cloud of witnesses; Grant that we, encouraged by the good examples of thy Saints, and especially of thy servant [Saint ——], may persevere in running the race that is set before us,

The Church Year

until at length, through thy mercy, we, with them, attain to thine eternal joy; through him who is the author and finisher of our faith, thy Son Jesus Christ our Lord. *Amen.*

Feast of the Dedication of a Church.

O GOD, whom year by year we praise for the dedication of this church; Hear, we beseech thee, the prayers of thy people, and grant that whosoever shall worship before thee in this place, may obtain thy merciful aid and protection; through Jesus Christ our Lord. *Amen.*

The Ember Days
At the Four Seasons.

O ALMIGHTY God, who hast committed to the hands of men the ministry of reconciliation; We humbly beseech thee, by the inspiration of thy Holy Spirit, to put it into the hearts of many to offer themselves for this ministry; that thereby mankind may be drawn to thy blessed kingdom; through Jesus Christ our Lord. *Amen.*

The Rogation Days
Being the Three Days before Ascension Day.

A LMIGHTY God, Lord of heaven and earth; We beseech thee to pour forth thy blessing upon this land, and to give us a fruitful season; that we, constantly receiving thy bounty, may evermore give thanks unto thee in thy holy Church; through Jesus Christ our Lord. *Amen.*

Independence Day.
[July 4.]

O ETERNAL God, through whose mighty power our fathers won their liberties of old; Grant, we beseech thee, that we and all the people of this land may have grace to maintain these liberties in righteousness and peace; through Jesus Christ our Lord. *Amen.*

Thanksgiving Day.

O MOST merciful Father, who hast blessed the labours of the husbandman in the returns of the fruits of the earth; We give thee humble and hearty thanks for this thy bounty; beseeching thee to continue thy loving-kindness to us, that our land may still yield her increase, to thy glory and our comfort; through Jesus Christ our Lord. *Amen.*

At a Marriage.

O ETERNAL God, we humbly beseech thee, favoura-bly to behold these thy servants now (*or* about to be) joined in wedlock according to thy holy ordinance; and grant that they, seeking first thy kingdom and thy right-eousness, may obtain the manifold blessings of thy grace; through Jesus Christ our Lord. *Amen.*

At the Burial of the Dead.

O ETERNAL Lord God, who holdest all souls in life; Vouchsafe, we beseech thee, to thy whole Church in paradise and on earth, thy light and thy peace; and grant that we, following the good examples of those who have served thee here and are now at rest, may at the last enter with them into thine unending joy; through Jesus Christ our Lord. *Amen.*

¶ *Or this.*

O GOD, whose mercies cannot be numbered; Accept our prayers on behalf of the soul of thy servant de-parted, and grant *him* an entrance into the land of light and joy, in the fellowship of thy saints; through Jesus Christ our Lord. *Amen.*

237-564-K-135-50

Illustrated by a Sister of the Community of the Holy Spirit.
The notes on Morning Prayer and Holy Communion were
prepared by Massey H. Shepherd, Jr., and
Robert N. Rodenmayer.

Our Prayers and Praise

For my son,

Thomas Alexander Lynch
Pennington, on the
occasion of his Christening
in the parish church of
St Paul, Flint Michigan.
10 November 1968.

Godparents:
the Rev. Frederick Robert Llovidson
Miss Elizabeth Barnhart
Mr. + Mrs. Gordon E. Gorkley

Jasper Green Pennington
Sewanee Tennessee